Australia

by Katie Bagley

Consultant:
Colleen Keen
Geography Department
Gustavus Adolphus College
St. Peter, Minnesota

Bridgestone Books

an imprint of Capstone Press
Mankato, Minnesota

Bridgestone Books are published by Capstone Press
151 Good Counsel Drive, P.O. Box 669, Mankato, Minnesota 56002
http://www.capstone-press.com

Library of Congress Cataloging-in-Publication Data
Bagley, Katie.
   Australia/by Katie Bagley.
   p. cm.—(Continents)
   Summary: Describes the regions, landforms, people, and interesting places of the
Australian continent.
   Includes bibliographical references and index.
   ISBN 0-7368-1417-5 (hardcover)
   1. Australia—Juvenile literature. [1. Australia.] I. Title. II. Continents (Mankato, Minn.)
DU96 .B34 2003
919.4—dc21
                                         2001007900

Editorial Credits

Erika Mikkelson, editor; Karen Risch, product planning editor; Linda Clavel, designer and
   illustrator; Image Select International, photo researchers

Photo Credits

Art Directors and TRIP/E. Smith, 15; Ask Images, 17; H. Rogers, 19; E. Smith, 22 (Lake Eyre)
CORBIS, 20, 22 (Great Barrier Reef)
Digital Stock, 18
Digital Wisdom/Mountain High, cover
Eye Ubiquitous/CORBIS, 22 (Uluru)
Paul A. Sonders/CORBIS, 13, 21
Rob Crandall/Stock Connection/PictureQuest, 11

1 2 3 4 5 6 07 06 05 04 03 02

Table of Contents

Fast Facts about Australia

Population: 19,357,594
(early 2000s estimate)

Number of independent nations: 1

Largest cities: Sydney, Melbourne, Brisbane, Perth

Capital city: Canberra

Longest river: Darling, 1,702 miles (2,739 kilometers)

Highest point: Mount Kosciusko, 7,310 feet (2,228 meters) above sea level

Lowest point: Lake Eyre, 52 feet (15.8 meters) below sea level

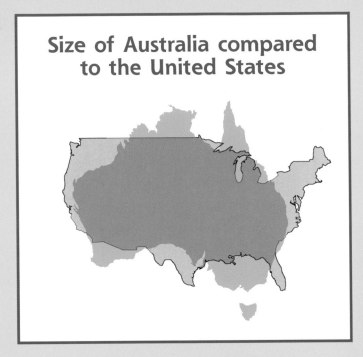

Size of Australia compared to the United States

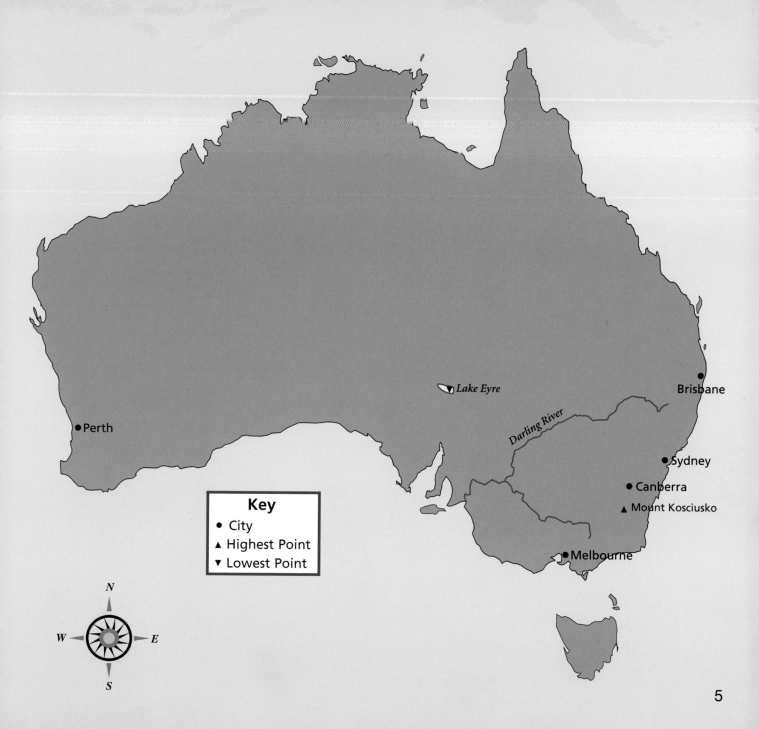

Key

● City
▲ Highest Point
▼ Lowest Point

▼ Lake Eyre

Darling River

● Perth

● Brisbane

● Sydney

● Canberra

▲ Mount Kosciusko

● Melbourne

N
W   E
S

Australia

Australia is the smallest continent. It is the largest island in a group of Pacific islands called Oceania. The Indian Ocean is to the west and south. The Tasman Sea and New Zealand lie to the southeast. Indonesia and Papua New Guinea lie to the north.

Oceania

an area of thousands of islands in the Pacific Ocean; New Zealand and Papua New Guinea are part of Oceania.

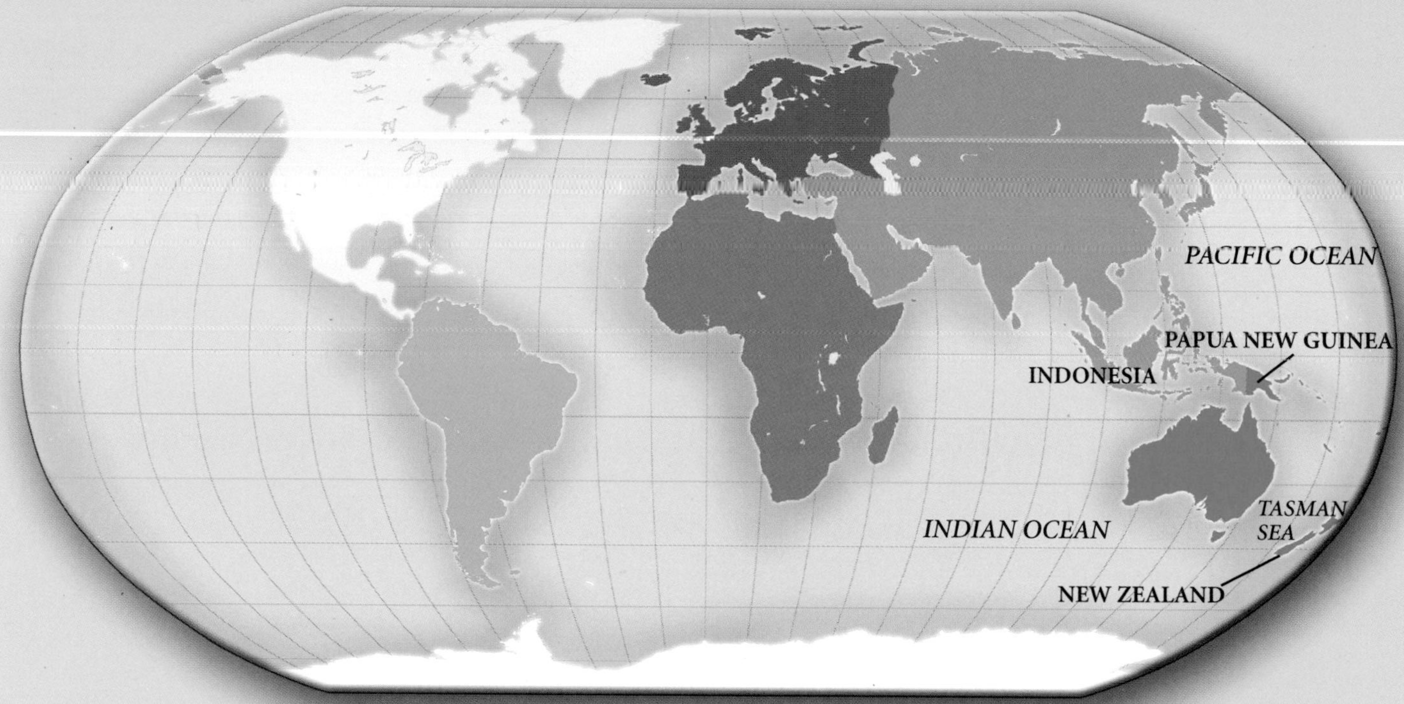
PACIFIC OCEAN
PAPUA NEW GUINEA
INDONESIA
INDIAN OCEAN
TASMAN SEA
NEW ZEALAND

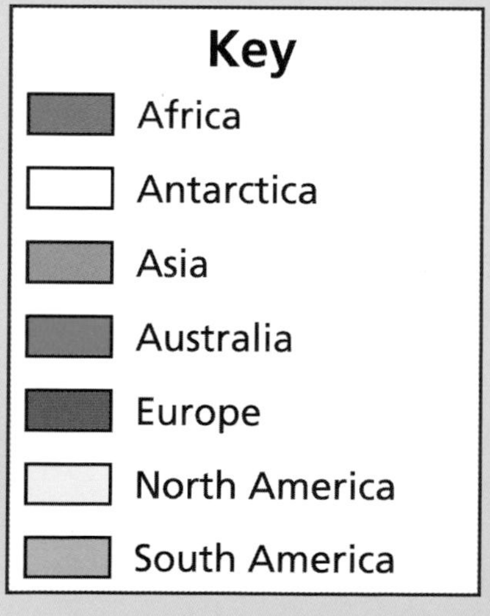
Key
Africa
Antarctica
Asia
Australia
Europe
North America
South America

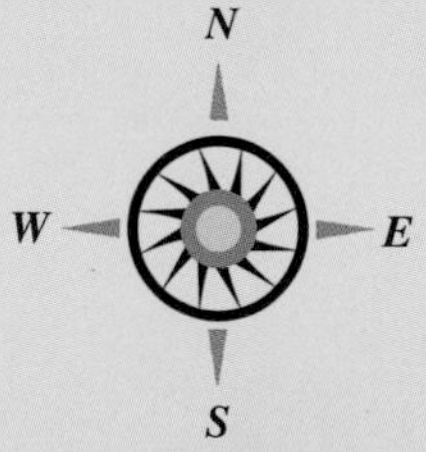
N
W
E
S

Australia's Land

Australia is the lowest and flattest continent. Deserts and grasslands lie in the middle of Australia. This area sometimes is called the Outback. The climate there is hot and dry. Rain forests grow in some areas along the coast of northeast Australia.

rain forest

a forest of tall trees that grows where the weather is warm and rainy all year

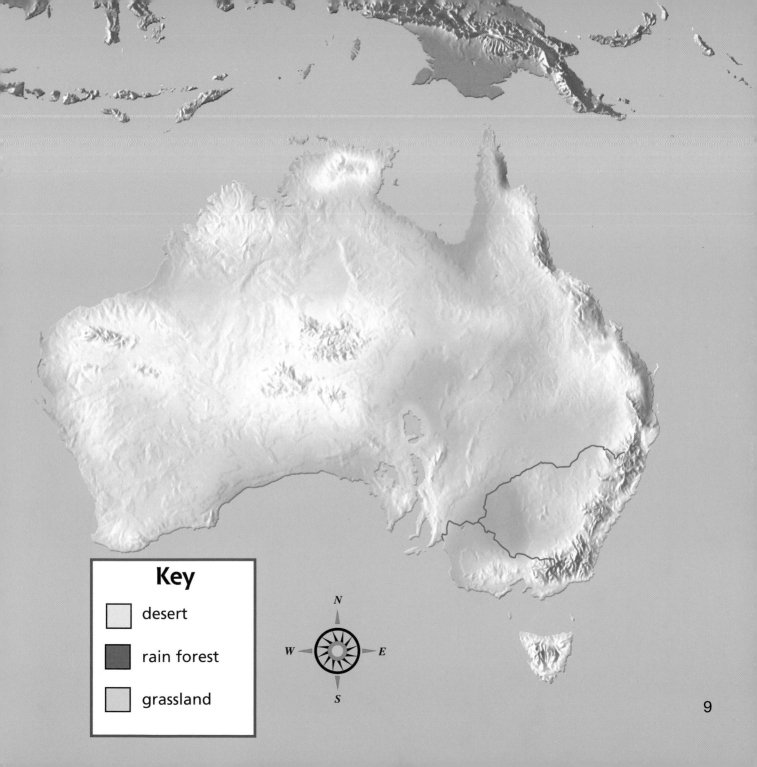

Key

desert

rain forest

grassland

N
W — E
S

9

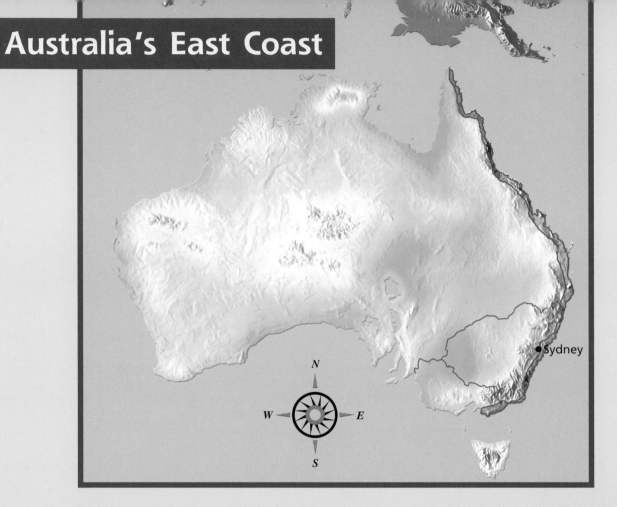

Low plains, sandy beaches, and rocky cliffs lie along Australia's east coast. This area receives more rainfall than other areas of the continent.

Sydney

Many people live in the cities on Australia's coast. Sydney is Australia's largest city. It was the site of the Olympic Games in 2000.

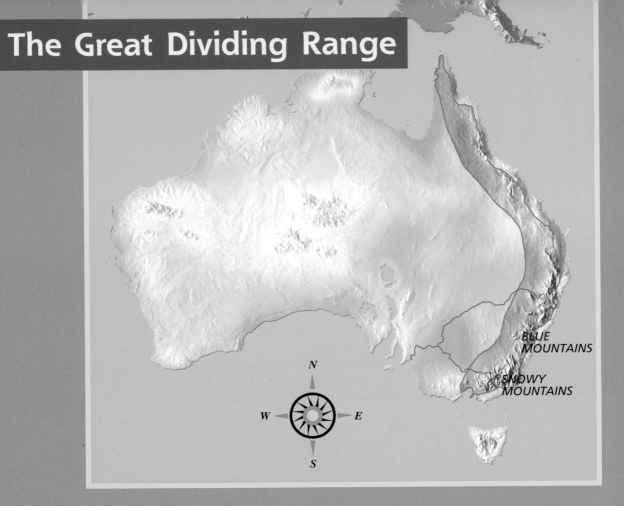

The Great Dividing Range separates the eastern coastal areas from the rest of the continent.

Three Sisters Rock, Blue Mountains National Park

The Great Dividing Range has high plateaus. The Blue Mountains and Snowy Mountains are in part of this range.

plateau
a raised area
of flat land

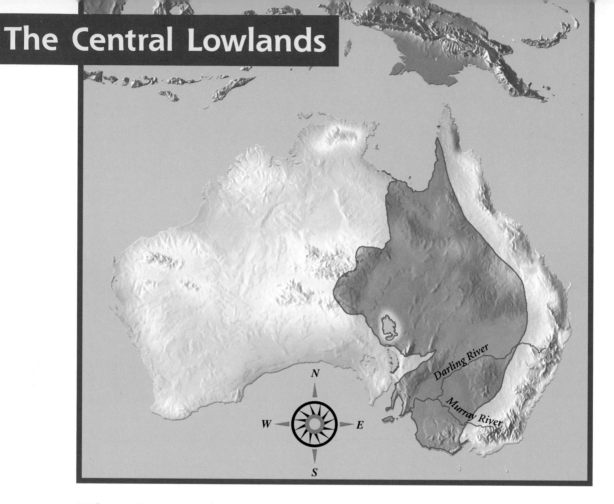

The Central Lowlands lie to the west of the Great Dividing Range. This area is hot and dry. The Darling River flows through this region.

Murray River

The Darling River empties into the
Murray River. Many people farm along
the Murray River.

The Western Plateau

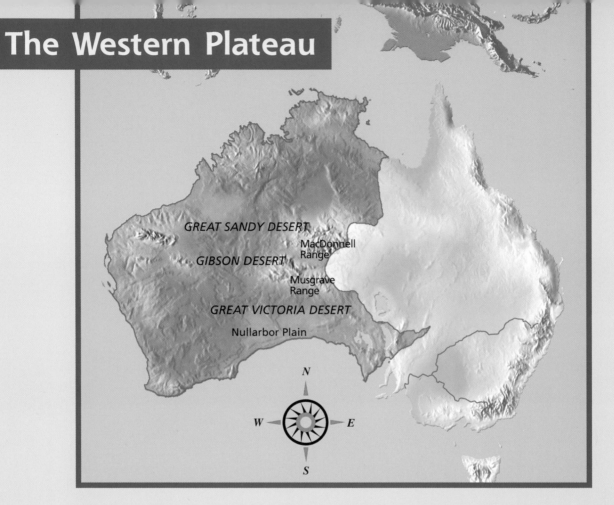

GREAT SANDY DESERT

MacDonnell Range

GIBSON DESERT

Musgrave Range

GREAT VICTORIA DESERT

Nullarbor Plain

N

W E

S

Australia's western half is a large plateau.
The Gibson Desert, Great Sandy Desert, and
Great Victoria Desert cover parts of this region.

Gibson Desert

The MacDonnell and Musgrave mountain ranges are in this region. The Nullarbor Plain runs along the region's southern edge.

Nullarbor Plain
a dry, flat area in Australia where few trees grow

17

kangaroo

Some kinds of Australian animals do not live anywhere else in the world. Kangaroos, koalas, and wombats are Australian marsupials.

marsupial

a type of animal that carries its young in a pouch on its body

kookaburra

Black swans, kookaburras, and emus are birds that live only in Australia. Emus run fast. But they cannot fly.

The country of Australia was once a British colony. Most Australians have British ancestors. About 4 percent of Australians are from Asia.

colony
land that is controlled
by another country

Aborigines make up 1 percent of Australians.
This group of people has lived in Australia
for more than 40,000 years.

Reading Maps: Australia's Sights to See

1. Uluru is the largest monolith in the world. This large stone is 6 miles (10 kilometers) around. Uluru is 1,143 feet (348 meters) tall. Is Uluru north or south of the Nullarbor Plain? Use the map on page 16 to answer this question.

2. The Great Barrier Reef is the largest coral reef in the world. The Great Barrier Reef is 1,250 miles (2,012 kilometers) long. Which way would you travel from Sydney, Australia, to find the Great Barrier Reef? Use the map on page 10 to answer this question.

3. Most of the natural lakes in Australia contain salt water. Lake Eyre is part of a system of salt lakes. The lakes used to be part of a large sea that dried up. Lake Eyre lies in which region? Is the Darling River to the east or west of Lake Eyre? Use the map on page 14 to answer these questions.

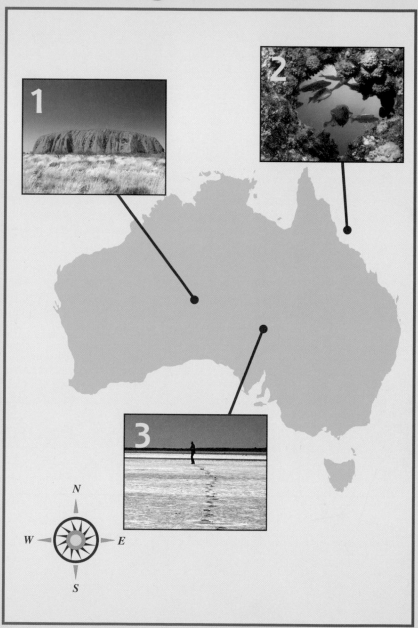

Words to Know

ancestor (AN-sess-tur)—a member of a family who lived a long time ago, such as a great-grandparent

continent (KON-tuh-nunht)—one of the seven large landmasses of Earth

coral reef (KOR-uhl REEF)—a strip of stony matter made up of the remains of small sea animals; a coral reef lies at or near the surface of water.

kookaburra (KUK-uh-bur-uh)—an Australian bird that makes a loud call that sounds like a person laughing

monolith (MON-oh-lith)—a single large stone

plain (PLANE)—a large, flat area of land

plateau (PLAH-toh)—a raised area of flat land

range (RAYNJ)—a chain or large group of mountains

wombat (WOM-bat)—a small bearlike animal

Read More

Grupper, Jonathan. *Destination: Australia.* Washington, D.C.: National Geographic Society, 2000.

Landau, Elaine. *Australia and New Zealand.* A True Book. New York: Children's Press, 1999.

Internet Sites

Australia Geography
http://www.kidport.com/RefLib/WorldGeography/Australia/
  Australia.htm
Australia: The Land and Its People
http://www.webweaver.com.au/australia
National Geographic on Australia
http://www.nationalgeographic.com/downunder

Index